Message Sent

Written by Mary-Anne Creasy

Flying Start
to Literacy®

T0363505

Contents

Introduction

People have always needed to send messages to each other.

Long ago, people did not have mobile phones, computers, television or radio. But they had many different ways of sending messages to each other.

Messages by relay

In the past, messages were often sent over long distances using horses or people.

Horse riders would carry messages and ride as fast as they could from one rest stop to the next.

At the rest stop, the rider would change to a fresh horse that was ready to run. This is called a relay.

By changing horses at each rest stop, riders were able to travel much faster than they could on one horse for the whole trip. One very famous horse relay was called the Pony Express.

The Incas were people who lived
in South America 600 years ago.
They did not have horses, so they
used people to send messages
in a relay.

Each runner would take the message and run to a rest stop where another runner would be waiting. The new runner would take the message and run on.

Runners carried messages along zig-zag paths up steep mountains.

Signals and flags

Long ago, people used smoke and flags to send messages.

Native Americans sent messages using smoke signals that could be seen far away.

To send a message by smoke signal, a damp blanket was placed over a fire for a short time. Puffs of smoke went into the air when the blanket was lifted up.

Each tribe used its own code to send messages so that its enemies would not understand the messages.

Flags on ships have been used to send messages for hundreds of years.

Each flag has a different pattern to represent a letter of the alphabet. The flags can be put together to spell words.

The flags on this ship's mast spell "birthday".

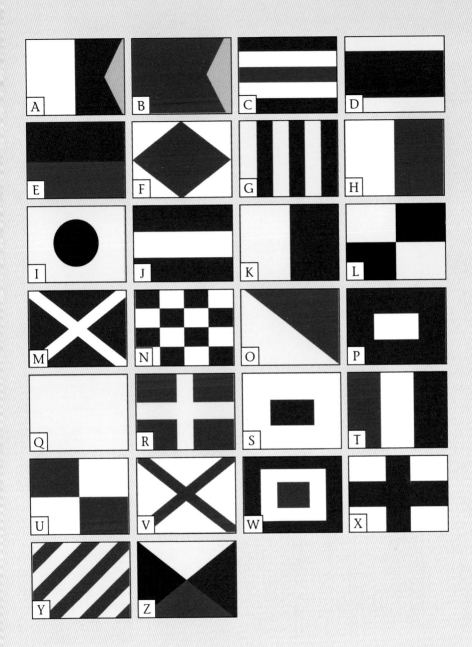

Each flag also sends a message when it is flown by itself.

The flag that represents the letter "p" is called the Blue Peter. When it is flown by itself, it tells people that the ship is about to sail.

Messages by sound

Sound can be used to send a message.

Long ago, Vikings sailed long distances in boats. Often their boats were too far away from each other for the Vikings to see signals.

They were able to send messages from one boat to another by blowing horns.

Drums have often been used to send messages.

The sound of the drums told the people that there was an enemy coming.

Today, at a school in Ghana in Africa, drums are used to send messages to the children.

The drum beats send them different messages such as "school is starting" or "come to a meeting".

Using animals to send messages

For thousands of years, pigeons have been used to carry messages. Pigeons can find their way home from faraway places.

Messages are written on paper and put into a tube on the pigeon's leg.

Dogs were also trained to carry
messages during battles. They were
good at carrying messages short
distances. They ran fast and could
easily get past enemy lines and go
places where a person could not go.

Then and now

People have always needed to send messages to each other, but the ways in which they send them have changed over time.

Today, we send messages electronically, using computers and mobile phones.

Messages can be sent in an instant to someone anywhere in the world.

Index